The Crab in the Crack

By Clem King

T0360268

A gull sat on some rocks.

Crang had a long bill.

He had black on his wings.

Crang looked for
some lunch.

He looked in the rocks.

"I can see a crab
in that crack!" Crang said.
"I love crabs!"

Peck! Stab!

"I will cram my bill down that crack!" said Crang.

"Go away, gull!" yelled Blip the crab. "Get off my home!"

Crang pecked, but the rocks blocked him.

He got very cross.

"You will not win!" yelled Blip.

"My bill can crush rocks!"
Crang said.

"Good luck, gull!" said Blip.
"Bills can not crush rocks!"

Crack!

But it was not rocks.

It was Crang's bill!

Crang did not get Blip!

CHECKING FOR MEANING

1. What colour were Crang's wings? *(Literal)*

2. Where did Crang look for lunch? *(Literal)*

3. Why did Blip love his home in the crack? *(Inferential)*

EXTENDING VOCABULARY

crab	Look at the word *crab*. How many letters are in this word? How many sounds are there?
crack	What sound does this word relate to in the story? Note that the word *crack* can be an action word (verb) or a naming word (noun). How is it used in this book?
crush	What does this word mean? What would big rocks look like if they were crushed?

MOVING BEYOND THE TEXT

1. What do you know about crabs? What do they eat? How do they protect themselves? What is their body covering?

2. What other animals do you know that have a shell to protect them?

3. Why do we often see gulls at the beach?

4. What other animals might a gull eat near the beach?

SPEED SOUNDS

bl	gl	cr	fr	st

PRACTICE WORDS

black

Crang

crab

Stab

crack

cram

blocked

Blip

Crack

crush